Laura

First Published 2023
© text Mari Lovgreen, 2023
© illustrations Sara Rhys, 2023

No part of this publication may be reproduced, stored in a retrieval system, or transmitted, in any form, or by any means, electrical, mechanical, photocopying, recording or otherwise without the prior permission of the publisher or a licence permitting restricted copying.

ISBN 978-1-914303-30-2

Published by Llyfrau Broga Books, Whitchurch, Cardiff

www.broga.cymru

Laura

The Stylish Life of Laura Ashley

Written by Mari Lovgreen
Illustrated by Sara Rhys

Laura Ashley was born in her grandmother's home in Merthyr Tydfil, South Wales.

Laura's dad was so happy to have a beautiful little girl, he bought her a present every day until her first birthday!

The family moved to London where noisy and lively little brothers and a sister were born.

When Laura was fourteen, the Second World War began.

The family travelled back to Wales to live with their grandmother.

Laura loved being in Wales - a beautiful place that was so different from London's crowded streets.

Here Laura learned what was most important to her: family, chapel and looking after her home.

A year later, Laura returned to London to help her father.

She went to college to learn to be a secretary before working with other women helping with the war effort.

Although she was a shy girl, she joined the local youth club. There she met a confident and exciting young man called Bernard Ashley.

They fell in love and were married in 1949.

Laura and Bernard were very poor but full of big ideas.

One thing that Laura really enjoyed was creating her own clothes. She taught herself how to print fabric with different patterns.

The couple bought a screen printer. Before long their house had become a busy little factory making clothes, scarves and other fabrics.

Laura took some of her scarves to a big store in London to try and sell them.

They proved so popular with customers that they sold out straight away, and she had to work through the nights to make more.

The business grew - and so did the family!

So that she could continue working, Laura would settle the children to bed at half past four in the afternoon.

Though she was becoming successful in London, Laura missed Wales. She decided to move her family to Machynlleth, a place close to her heart.

A shop and factory was soon opened in nearby Carno.

This created lots of much-needed jobs for local people, and Laura treated all her staff as family.

Laura came up with a new idea, to create long, comfortable dresses with flowery patterns.

Very quickly, the word spread and the world fell in love with her unique designs.

Everyone wanted to wear her clothes!

The company grew and grew until there was over a thousand staff, three factories, forty shops - and even a jet plane!

Laura Ashley stores opened all over the world - from London to New York, Paris to Australia.

Her designs were used for wallpaper and furniture fabrics as well as clothes.

Though the company was now worth millions, taking care of her family, her home and her staff was always more important to Laura than business success.

Laura died suddenly just before her sixtieth birthday.

Despite their great sadness, people from Carno and all over the world came together to celebrate her wonderful life.

Laura Ashley is still widely remembered as a big-hearted woman whose creativity and business sense combined to make the world a more beautiful place.

Read about more
Welsh Wonders

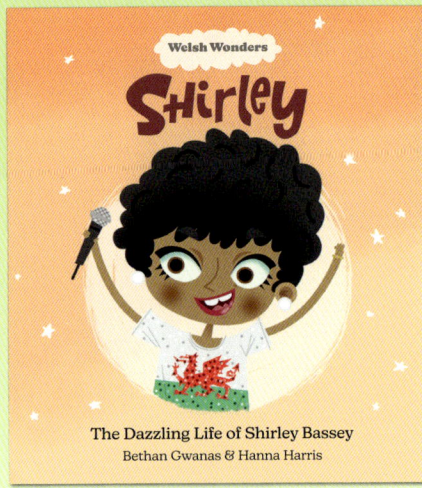

Shirley Bassey
The girl from Tiger Bay whose voice became famous around the world.

Cranogwen
Sarah Jane Rees was a sea captain, prize-winning poet, publisher, and inspiration!

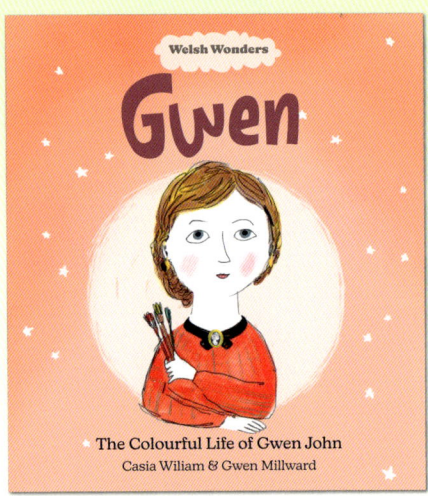

Gwen John
A shy but determined girl who loved to paint and followed her dream of being a famous artist.

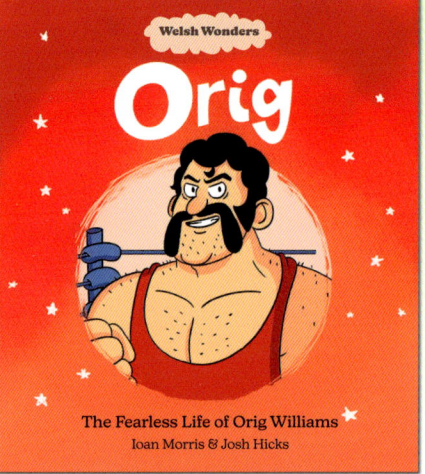

Orig Williams
The tough-guy wrestler with a heart of gold, known around the world as El Bandito!

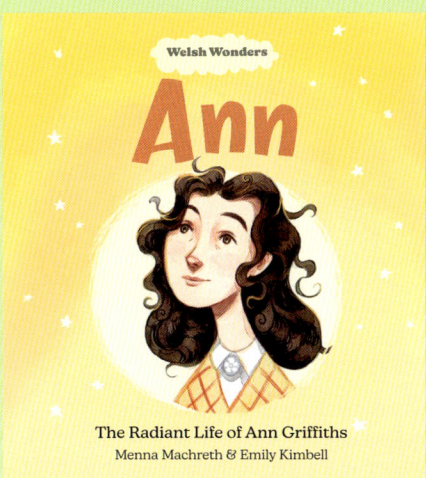

Ann Griffiths
The sensitive poet whose spiritual songs inspired millions.

Aneurin Bevan
Inspirational politician who founded the NHS and changed a nation.

Coming soon...

Betty Campbell
The inspirational story of Wales' first Black headteacher, who fought for equality and fairness in education.

Alfred Russel Wallace
The adventurous naturalist who travelled the world and made incredible discoveries.

Find out more about other inspiring Welsh lives – from artists and scientists to people who challenged the way things were and overcame difficulties to achieve their dreams.